PRAYERS
FUTURE H~~~~~~~

100 Inspirational Prayers

BY

MELONIE SMITH

PUBLISHED BY

KRATOS PUBLISHERS

All bible Scripture quotations Authorized King James version

Published in 1769 public domain

ISBN: 9781097319244

**PUBLISHED BY
KRATOS PUBLISHERS**

CONTENT

WAITING

so as to walk in a manner worthy of the Lord, fully pleasing to him: bearing fruit in every good work and increasing in the knowledge of God;

being strengthened with all power, according to his glorious might, for all endurance and patience with joy;

Colossians 1: 10- 11 (KJV)

I felt like I have been waiting on you for a life time, but I will continue to wait until God has said yes; these two shall become one.

PRAYER 1

I pray that wherever you are, the Lord will keep you in perfect peace right now, may your heart not be troubled. May the peace of God that surpasses all understanding continue to keep your heart and mind at rest in Jesus Name. May your side, body, immune system be in good health. May all your organs function immaculately.

MIDNIGHT THOUGHT

When I remember thee upon my bed, and meditate on thee in the night watches. Because thou hast been my help, therefore in the shadow of thy wings will I rejoice.

My soul followeth hard after thee: thy right hand upholdeth me.

Psalms 63:6-8 (KJV)

I think of you through the night as I lay on my bed.

PRAYER 2

May you always meditate on God's word as you lay on your bed, may your thoughts think about God's goodness and mercy as you lay your head to rest at night, may the angel of the Lord continue to watch over you always.

May you have good dreams, may your sleep be sweet, may the angel of the Lord visit you as you sleep, may you have beautiful and heavenly visions, may you experience even the very tangible presence of God as you lay your head to rest and as you arise in the morning, be still and know your God is with you always. You are never alone.

WELLNESS

Surely he has borne our griefs and carried our sorrows; yet we esteemed him stricken, smitten by God, and afflicted. But he was pierced for our transgressions; he was crushed for our iniquities; upon him was the chastisement that brought us peace, and with his wounds we are healed.

Isaiah 53: 4-5 (KJV)

PRAYER 3

*M*y prayer for you today is that you will be well

in mind, body, soul and Spirit. May the Lord grant you peace, in all that you do today. May your body be in good health and strength.

I pray that no accident will befall you, no force of darkness will overshadow you. May your footsteps be ordered by the Lord.

May all your body parts function in the way it was designed to operate.

I pray that whatsoever you put your hands to will prosper. May your plans and visions come to past.

May He heal every broken bone and heart aches. Be strong in the power of the Lord.

FALLING IN LOVE

Delight yourself in the LORD, and he will give you the desires of your heart.

Psalms 37:4 (KJV)

I keep falling in love with you over and over again, my dearest husband- I write this diary entry with you in my mind, I miss you and I can't wait to share our lives together. As we prepare in this season of waiting.

PRAYER 4

May our hearts, mind, soul and body be

under the leading of the Holy Spirit. In all our ways may we acknowledge Him, and He will be sure to direct our path, let's continue to commit our ways unto the Lord.

He knows the way we should go, may this month be a time of fulfilled potential and favour in Jesus name, May the Joy of the Lord be our strength today and always.

POWER OF THE CROSS

And behold, the curtain of the temple was torn in two, from top to bottom. And the earth shook, and the rocks were split.

Matthew 27:51 (KJV)

PRAYER 5

I pray that you will forever know the power

and symbolism of Jesus' death on the cross. May your heart always be on the things of God. May you never be overwhelmed but always know that Jehovah desires for you to have perfect communion with him.

May the spirit of the Lord be in everything you do, on this journey that you are on. As we prepare ourselves for God's perfect will and destiny for our lives. May we be ready to accept and receive each other in our lives, becoming one for the betterment of God's kingdom and fulfilling His perfect will.

LOVE SONGS

Addressing one another in psalms and hymns and spiritual songs, singing and making melody to the Lord with your heart,

Ephesians 5: 19 (KJV)

Let us speak to each other in love, hymns, psalms and spiritual songs.

PRAYER 6

*H*eavenly Father- I pray that if there are disagreements and concerns between my future husband and I, we will not judge each other falsely.

I pray that there will be a spirit of honesty, love, respect and self-acceptance. I come against every word that is intended to hurt and destroy.

May you speak with a sense of conviction, correction and humility.

May you always remember that no one is perfect, and everyone deserves a second chance. May we be able to hold hands and pray at the end of our disagreements in Jesus name.

14

OVERCOMING SIN

Therefore, since we are surrounded by so great a cloud of witnesses, let us also lay aside every weight, and sin which clings so closely, and let us run with endurance the race that is set before us,

Hebrews 12: 1 (KJV)

PRAYER 7

*M*y dearest,

I pray that we will lay aside everything that will cause us to stray from the presence and will of our Almighty. I pray that wherever you are today. Your mind will be at peace.

I pray that the enemy will not have any stronghold over your life. May you cast all your cares upon Jehovah, knowing that he cares for you today, tomorrow and always. May you live a victorious life, knowing that God is fighting all your battles, and He has overcome every sin known to man.

Therefore, your victory is sure in Jesus Christ name. live, pray and worship from a position of victory.

GIFTS OF GOD

As every man hath received the gift, even so minister the same one to another, as good stewards of the manifold grace of God. If any man speak, let him speak as the oracles of God; if any man minister, let him do it as of the ability which God giveth: that God in all things may be glorified through Jesus Christ, to whom be praise and dominion for ever and ever. Amen.

1 Peter 4: 10 -11 (KJV)

Prayer 8

*M*y dear, God has given to you; special abilities.

May you use them to help each other. May the Lord enable you to see and promote Godly character in those dearest and closest to you.

May you be the eyes that sees the spots that I have missed, may you be a prayer partner- may you be my right hand, when my left hand is engaged and unable to reach for my left.

I pray that the peace and power of the Almighty will be upon your lips, when you pray and minister with the love of God.

SUFFERING

For in that he himself hath suffered being tempted, he is able to succour them that are tempted.

Hebrews 2: 18 (KJV)

Prayer 9

May we always know that God will allow us

to go through certain situations, so that, when we speak, witness, share and evangelize, we do so with an authority that can not be discredited, because it is our experience.

My dear, may you be mindful that your experiences, whether great, small, hurtful, disappointing, successful or sorrowful, remember that God is working all things, for the good of those who love him.

There might be times in our journey where, even your very own, the closest and dearest to you will disappoint or might unintentionally cause you distress, but remember Jesus came to his own and his own did not receive Him. Always rest assured that you have a great high priest who can understand the feelings of your infirmities. I pray that you will have the spirit of Job when he echoed, "when he hath tried

me, I shall come forth as gold". (Job 23:10)
(KJV)

God will give you a revelation of His glory,
when you sometimes try to share it with your
own; they might not even believe or take you
seriously, but do not be discouraged, you are
not seeking to please man but God. It is better
to please God than to please man.

He will be our ultimate judge. I pray that you
will have a supportive lifestyle with your
helpmate in ministry and spirit.

May you share in the vision of God's
immaculate grace and power. May you be
emotionally and spiritually intelligent to the
needs of your soul mate, (partner, wife and
helpmate) may we both develop an
understanding that is unique to our
relationship and our ministry in Jesus name.

GOODNESS AND MERCY

Surely goodness and mercy shall follow me all the days of my life: and I will dwell in the house of the LORD for ever.

Psalms 23: 6 (KJV)

Prayer 10

I pray that the angel of the Lord will always encamp around you, wherever you go, may the Joy of the Lord always be your strength. May your body be well and healthy. May good health always be your portion. May you look after your body, mind, soul and prayer life.

May you do things in moderation. May you have a sense of discernment for all that God has placed in you, may you become an avid reader, may our children see us as readers, may our children be outstanding children, who are humble, talented and easy to love, may they be leaders in their generation.

May we live in harmony, may we play around, joke around and always be in love with each other. Even when we upset each other, may we forgive and make up quickly.

May we be excited and feel that we are fully blessed to have found each other.

May we value our relationship, may we value what God has given to us, may we abide under the covering of the Almighty God. I Cannot wait to start our life together.

Love always,

Your future wife.

PRAYING MAN

Men ought to always to pray and not to faint.

Luke 18: 1b (KJV)

I woke up with a desire to pray, to consecrate myself before our throne of Grace.

Prayer 11

*H*eavenly Father, I pray that your mighty hand

of approval will be upon all our thoughts, emotions and decisions in our lives today and always.

May you always be a man of prayer because, with prayer comes power to live the victorious life in Jesus Christ.

May you be a man of integrity, may your word precede you, may you be known for your words and cautiousness, may you pray in the spirit and prophetically to offer healing, deliverance, breakthrough and liberty in Jesus Christ, using the power of intercession of His Holy words, Amen.

PERSEVERING IN PROMISE

Cast not away therefore your confidence, which hath great recompense of reward.

Hebrews 10: 35 (KJV)

Prayer 12

*L*ike Abraham, may you hold on to God's

promises in season and out of season. May you repeat the promises of God daily over your life, even when the situation speaks or maybe dictating otherwise, hold on to the confidence of God's undiluted words.

Like Daniel, Shadrack, Meshach and Abednego, hold on to the confidence and word of God, where you can stand and say boldly; Even if my God refuses to hear me "you" I will not bow.

Trust God, when everything and your situation around you looks different and may appear silly to the world, when logic says; pack up and run, give up, change your thinking cap but, may you be unmovable like Simon, who is able to remind God of His promises and your continued obedience to His word.

PURPOSEFUL DESTINY

Dear future husband

Prayer 13

May you be an encourager, my cheer
leader, confidant, protector and the eyes
behind my back.

Heavenly Father, I ask you to cover this man
right now, the man that you have ordained for
me, before our existence to be together.

Where we can truly fulfil your purpose and
perfect will for our lives, may you take charge
over every thought in Jesus name.

DAILY INCREASE

Give, and it shall be given unto you; good measure, pressed down, and shaken together, and running over, shall men give into your bosom. For with the same measure that ye mete withal it shall be measured to you again.

Luke 6:38 (KJV)

Prayer 14

Heavenly Father,

I pray that we will learn to be kind and honest

with each other daily, may we see the initial start to our marriage life together, as an empty suitcase; where it can be filled with qualities that will sustain and keep a healthy, strong, successful and impactful marriage.

Dear Lord, may we understand that we have the ability to create the type of life that we desire for each other where our lives will become one. Therefore, may we learn to invest in our relationship.

May we seek to develop a greater understanding of acquired knowledge, through reading, sharing encouraging, challenging and bettering ourselves, so we can be the best version of who we are meant to be in Jesus name.

POWER OF LOVE

Love never gives up. Love cares more for others than for self. Love doesn't want what it doesn't have. Love doesn't strut, Doesn't have a swelled head, Doesn't force itself on others, isn't always "me first," doesn't fly off the handle, doesn't keep score of the sins of others, doesn't revel when others grovel, takes pleasure in the flowering of truth, puts up with anything, Trusts God always, always looks for the best, never looks back, but keeps going to the end.

1 Corinthians 13:4-8a (MSG)

Prayer 15

Dear Husband,

*M*ay these endless qualities of love be permeated through your bone, body and thought in Jesus name.

May you first and foremost experience this unconditional love, – where you will be able to return or offer it freely in return, as you would have known the liberation and victory that it brings.

May our lives be one of victorious love. May we continue in loving each other, as first love in Jesus name, Amen

CONFIDENCE IN CHRIST JESUS

Heavenly Father

I pray that my future husband will not be disturbed in his view of your unconditional love and value of his life.

May he know that what he does- does not reflect (God's) Your purpose and view of him.

What he does is not a reflection of who he is – when you fall – may you know that God is always there, waiting for you to return to him with a repented heart. May you always know that Christ has redeemed you; you are righteous through Jesus Christ.

May you know always that you are the righteousness of God. Greater is He that lives in you! May you know that you are chosen. May you know that you are an heir of God's family. May you know that the weapon of your warfare is not carnal but mighty, through the pulling down of strong holds in Jesus name.

TRAVEL PROTECTION

Prayer 17

May the Lord watch over you as you travel, may He watch over your going out and your coming in, from the moment you enter in a new country.

May protection be upon your travels to and from the airport, may the angel of the Lord be the airwave and in the wind. May you experience the awesome presence of your creator as you see His wonders and a new insight of His creation as you fly and drive.

May you take the name of the Lord with you everywhere you go. May you not forget the promises that you have vowed in your heart, to honour the Lord your God with all your heart, mind, soul and body.

Be strong in the Lord and the power of God's thought. Continue to put on the whole armour that you may be able to stand in the day of trouble.

CREATED WORKMANSHIP

For we are His workmanship created to do His Good work

Ephesians 2:10(KJV)

*H*eavenly Father, this is the day that you have made, – May my Husband always rejoice and be glad in every single day that you have made and will permit him to see and experience your glory.

Thank you, Father, for sparing his life for over four decades. Thank you, Father, for allowing him to be in his right mind. Thank you for allowing him to have favour in you. Thank you for allowing him to be part of your kingdom.

Father please do for my husband this year what nobody else will be able to do. May you order his steps from the rising of the sun to the going down. Continue to cover and watch over his decisions all the days of his life. For He is your handiwork, oh Lord! – So, take delight in him.

Like an open book, you watch him grow and mature into a man, from conception to birth; all the stages of his life were spread out before you Lord, the days of his life all prepared before you.

LET'S DO IT RIGHT

"I don't want that... Now if you want to marry me, let's do this right. Let's pledge ourselves to each other."

Let us not chase after what is cheap that is without commitment. Let us not seek to satisfy our desires for the spur of the moment and grief the Holy Spirit.

May the God of Abraham speak clearly to us: about our "intimacy with Jesus Christ, – out of our intimacy with Jesus Christ will come forth true revival"

"the babies of revival are from granite rock of commitment to the Bridegroom. Babies are always birthed from intimacy".

God Chaser pg. 129"

Prayer 19

*H*eavenly Father

I praise your name right now as I read your book, God Chaser and study this chapter "All they want to do is date God", it causes me to reflect on my life and wonder, if]we are mirroring this in our relationship.

Father, may we profess that which you require of us. May we always present our mind, body and spirit before you as a living sacrifice. Holy and acceptable unto you, which is our reasonable service, dear Lord.

Heavenly Father may our relationship with each other be not for convenience, but may we be serious in our commitment. Lord, I pray that he will be ready, committed and ready to seek after true intimacy with you, then emulate that example in his natural relationship that we share.

Lord, please let this be done in due time not according to my will, but your will in Jesus name.

Lord, I know that our thoughts are not your thoughts neither are your ways ours – but let this not be a man-made delay in your name.

Please give Him the urge and zeal to make things in order, so we can truly begin true intimacy with each other. We can be effective procreators and ambassadors for you in your name I pray.

Please help us to cultivate a rooted relationship with you together as a couple, friend, church brother and sister before we can become intimate. Where we will be able to maintain and sustain this long living intimacy for the rest of our life, through continued development and growth in the word.

Father, may we always find and have our commitment in you.

"children are by products of their household". May we produce beautiful, God loving, compassionate, passionate, radical children who change the world for God's kingdom.

May we love you and honour you always with our body, life, money and servitude, dear Lord in Jesus name.

SAFE JOURNEY

For he shall give his angels charge over thee,
to keep thee in all thy ways.

Psalms 91:11(KJV)

Prayer 20

*H*eavenly Father, I ask for your divine

protection on every area of his travel, right now in Jesus name. May you clear every trap and hinderances that is not from you.

May whatsoever the enemy have in store against you be cancelled and thwarted.

May you have a testimony to share at the end of your travel, this one in particular. May there be a divine impartation and revelation of your destiny.

God, you want to use us for a higher level in you. May we be ready to adhere to the divine purpose of God's will. May we not question the hands of God in all that we do.

Thank you, Jehovah, for journey mercies.
Amen.

FINANCIAL WISDOM

Prayer 21

Heavenly Father, I praise your Holy Name.

Thank you for answering prayers, thank you that you know every thought before they are uttered.

Lord, I pray that my future husband will have discipline over his financial affair. I pray that he will use wisdom and not pride in his spending. Lord, may he be a good steward of our money. May we be a good steward of our money and all you have placed in our care.

I pray that the canker worm will not devour the fruit of our labour. I pray that financial freedom will be his and our destiny.

Lord, you said whatsoever we desire when we pray, we should believe. Lord, you said we should write down our vision and make it plain. So, dear Lord may your perfect will be fulfilled.

May we talk and agree about your visions for our lives. Lord, may there be a spirit of completion in our lives, so we can progress to the next level in Jesus name. Heavenly Father, may your grace and mercy continue to abide with us.

DIVINE ORDER

Prayer 22

Heavenly Father, may your order always be in our plans. May we always have you at the forefront of all that we do and say.

Lord, if there is anything in our lives that displeases you, please show us. In Jesus name.

EMOTIONAL INTELLIGENCE

Prayer 23

*H*eavenly Father, I pray that my future husband will be able to understand my emotional intelligence and understand my emotions when situations arises.

I pray that we will be able to understand each other's point to agree, acknowledge and value each other's perspective, Lord, I pray that anger, wrath and sentiment will not be our portion.

May you speak through our anger, cause us not to sin in our wrath. May we both express ourselves carefully and respectfully.

May we speak through the situation, then pray and leave everything at your altar. Help us to listen, be slow to speak and quick to listen in Jesus name.

May hurtful memories of the past not wake the sentiment and anger in our hearts in Jesus name.

COMMUNICATION

Prayer 24

*D*ear Lord, sometimes I feel like when I need

to speak to the person who I believe is meant
to be the most important person and when
they are nowhere to be found then it can
create a barrier to effective communication.

Heavenly Father, please help me to listen, plan
and create plans according to progress meant.

Lord, please help my other half to understand
my concerns and the things that affect one's
future. I dislike inconsistency in relationship.
Thank you for hearing in Jesus name.

PATIENT REGULATION

Prayer 25

Lord Jesus, I pray that I will learn to regulate my emotions. May your thoughts be in me. Please, help me to meditate on your promise for my future husband and my future life soul mate.

Lord, right now I sense frustration and disappointment, as I can't really see any way forward. I am not seeing any visible changes or progress in preparation for a life where two are becoming one.

Heavenly Father, please help me to regulate my desires. May you truly lead me to your heart beat for me. I know you want what is best for me. So please if it is not the best for me. Withhold it and give me a sense of peace and always to understand that you truly are working things out for my good in Jesus name.

PERFECT LOVE

There is no fear in love; but perfect love casteth out fear:

1 John 4:18a (KJV)

Prayer 26

*H*eavenly Father I come to you right now

asking you to create in me a clean heart and a right spirit.

Lord I give you thanks for small mercies. I pray that you will heal every broken heart. Heal weary, heavy and contrite heart, oh God.

Every emotion that is a lie and differs from the truth Lord. I pray that you will be exalted in this relationship Lord.

May every proud spirit be subjected under your feet in Jesus name.

May truth be seen and every lie cast out.

HUMILITY

Prayer 27

Heavenly Father, please help us to humble ourselves, so that you can exalt us. Help us to say I'm sorry. Help us to stay on our knees until you give us the green light. May your direction always be with us.

I speak to every doubt, I speak to every fear, I speak to every disappointment, I speak to every lie, I speak to anxiety, I speak to every trial, I speak to every pain. I thank you for your deliverance, healing and restoration.

I will bless you at all times, your praise shall continue to be in our mouth. Let's Magnify the Lord together and bless His Holy name.

Flood our hearts with your works of deliverance and breakthrough Lord.

SECURED FUTURE

Prayer 28

Lord, if there are any stumbling blocks that will cause issues in the future that isn't in line with your promises. I pray that you will reveal them now, Holy Spirit, so they can be dealt with. In Jesus name. Father I pray that you will reveal your timely ways.

May every anxiety, uncertainty and fear be cast down right now in the name of Jesus.

Lord, I decrease, and you must increase. Help me to humble myself in this season – when we humble ourselves. The Lord will exalt us but if we exalt ourselves the Lord will humble us.

So, dear Father grant me humility and wisdom in you. May I not be making silly decisions and thinking that I'm doing something wonderful. Please order my steps in your word dear Lord. Please help me to balance my emotions when it comes to hearing, seeing, sensing and preparing for the future.

CLEAR WAYS

I will go before thee, and make the crooked places straight: I will break in pieces the gates of brass, and cut in sunder the bars of iron:

Isa 45:2(KJV)

Prayer 29

*H*eavenly Father please help my future soul mate to see himself clearly and make positive changes and choices in life. One that will draw him closer to fulfil the purpose you have designed for him.

Lord, may every crooked path become straight and clear in Jesus name.

Lord, may every high wall be broken down. Take every fear and cast it into the sea of forgetfulness.

I pray that he will have the right attitude and approach to disappointment and success. May you order our steps dear Lord. Lead me, guide me every day.

Send your anointing Father we pray on our lives.

LOVE LETTER

Love letter from God to my Husband.

Prayer 30

*H*usband, you have a relationship with me but I seek you to know me more. I know everything there is to know about you because I've created you before you were woven together in your mother's womb. Even the single hair on your head are all counted and numbered. For in me you live, move, drive, talk and have your being.

You are my offspring. I chose you from the beginning. I know your ending. I have chosen you, your life is not a mistake. You are fearfully and wonderfully made. I designed every part of your body the way I meant it to be designed. There is no mistake in your physical features when I created you. You are my special son.

I am the complete expression of love and forgiveness. People have misrepresented and misunderstood me. But I am God of justice.

It is my desire to lavish my love and favour on you. Simply because you are my (child) son. I am your Father. I am the perfect Father.

Every good gift that you receive comes from my hand. For I am your provider and I meet all your needs according to my riches in glory.

My plan for your future has always been with hope. I'm a God of love and my gift for you is an everlasting love. My thoughts towards you are countless and I rejoice over you with singing – I will never stop doing good for you, for you Oh Husband, are my treasured possession.

I desire to establish you with all my heart and soul.

I want to show you great and marvellous things. If you truly seek me with all your heart, all your mind, all your understanding and all your ways, then you will truly find me waiting to fill you up.

Continue to delight in me – take pleasure in serving me and I will surely give you the desires of your heart, for it is I who created these desires. Remember that eyes have not seen, ears have not heard the plans that I have for those who trust, obey and love me. I am able to do far exceedingly more than you can ever think or imagine. I am your God. For

I am your greatest encourager. I am your Father.

Find all the encouraging words that I have left for you in my words. May your mind always be upon my unfailing love and promises for you. Speak over yourself.

I am your Father, friend, comforter who comforts you when you are troubled, when your heart is broken, when the world is unfair. I love you even as I love my son Jesus, you are my world. For in Jesus my love for you is revealed.

He came to show you my love, His death is the ultimate expression of my love for you.

Nothing will be able to separate you from my love. Nothing, nothing will be able to separate you from my unfailing love.

Go and live in the expression of my promises, my love, my victory, my power. For no good thing will I withhold from those who truly desire the things after my own heart.

I love you son!

SPIRIT AND TRUTH

Behold, I will do a new thing; now it shall spring forth; shall ye not know it? I will even make a way in the wilderness, and rivers in the desert.

Isaiah 43:19 (KJV)

Prayer 31

Heavenly Father, I thank you for one more day. I bless your name for leading me through the prayer session at church. I pray that your spirit will continue to penetrate through every dark corner and difficult period of our lives.

May your Spirit and truth continue to see through my future husband and I relationship.

Dear Lord, please help us to understand your truth and your way for our lives. Lord, please help us to be wise in your will for the plans you have for us.

RECEIVING TOGETHER

The Lord called Samuel, Samuel answered. "Here I am"

1 Samuel 3:4   (KJV)

Prayer 32

*H*eavenly Father as we prepare to attend this worship dance conference together, please prepare our hearts in such a special way, that it will be open up to receive fresh revelation and confirm that which you require from both of us in fulfilling our God given purpose on this earth.

Please help us to truly surrender our personal desires to your leading and direction for our lives, so that you can have your perfect way in us.

EYE OPENER

Prayer 33

*H*eavenly Father,

Thank you for provision and protection. Thank you for showing My future husband, a glimpse of some of the works involved in this ministry.

Thank you that he was able to attend and fellowship in worship. Thank you for giving him a fresh eye opener into the dance ministry. May all your purposes and will for his life be fulfilled in Jesus name.

Heavenly Father, thank you for all the people my friends and dance worshippers that he had the opportunity to meet over the weekend. Lord, may we continue to learn and understand each other emotional and spiritual wellbeing in Jesus name.

WISE BUILDER

Therefore whosoever heareth these sayings of mine, and doeth them, I will liken him unto a wise man, which built his house upon a rock: And the rain descended, and the floods came, and the winds blew, and beat upon that house; and it fell not: for it was founded upon a rock. And every one that heareth these sayings of mine, and doeth them not, shall be likened unto a foolish man, which built his house upon the sand: And the rain descended, and the floods came, and the winds blew, and beat upon that house; and it fell: and great was the fall of it.

Matthew 7:24-27 (KJV)

Prayer 34

The wise and foolish builders:

Heavenly Father, I pray that my future husband will hear the word and put it into practice, like a wise man who built his house on the rock.

May our relationship be built on your foundation. Lord, where we set your standard on the way to cover our lives.

Lord, may when the storm of lives comes to blow us down... May we stand firm on your word of power and assurance that you are working out things for our good.

As the rain comes down, the stream rises, the wind blows and beat against the house, but may it always stand.

Lord, may our faith and assurance in you be unshakeable in Jesus name.

Lord, as we prepare for building a life together, we declare all your promises over our lives in Jesus name, Amen.

PERFECT MAN

For in many things we offend all. If any man offend not in word, the same *is* a perfect man, *and* able also to bridle the whole body.

James 3:2 (KJV)

Prayer 35

*H*eavenly Father, I pray that your spirit will always convict my future husband when he is experiencing a dark point in his walk with you where he needs to hear you clearly.

May when he falls, he always find the grace and strength to rise up and be determined to trust, dust off the (ground) dirt, receive your abundant grace and walk in victory knowing that there is no condemnation to those who are in you Lord Jesus.

Heavenly Father, may he always know that you are not condemning him Lord and that your grace is sufficient, for each and every desert place in the wilderness.

May you always be the glaring light that propels us to live in victory through Him, who strengthens us, Amen.

EYES ON THE LORD

Mine eyes are ever toward the LORD; for he shall pluck my feet out of the net. Turn thee unto me, and have mercy upon me; for I am desolate and afflicted. The troubles of my heart are enlarged: O bring thou me out of my distresses.

Psalm 25: 15-17 (KJV)

Prayer 36

*H*eavenly Father, May my future husband's eyes forever be upon you. May you guide and strengthen his heart so he can be comforted in time of distress and anguish.

Heavenly Father you are his Father, please soften his heart from the pain and cares of this day. May he abide under the shadow of your Almighty love.

May he find grace and peace in troubled times. May your word give him a new sense of hope and victory in you. Lord, may the word grant him favour and access to your presence.

May his request be made known to you. May you give him knowledge, wisdom and understanding to keep your word in his heart.

ALL DILIGENCE

And beside this, giving all diligence, add to your faith virtue; and to virtue knowledge; And to knowledge temperance; and to temperance patience; and to patience Godliness; And to Godliness brotherly kindness; and to brotherly kindness charity.

For if these things be in you, and abound, they make you that ye shall neither be barren nor unfruitful in the knowledge of our Lord Jesus Christ. But he that lacketh these things is blind, and cannot see afar off, and hath forgotten that he was purged from his old sins.

2peter 1:5-9(KJV)

Prayer 37

Heavenly Father, I thank you for small mercies Lord, please, forgive us when we fall short of your promises and expectations for us Lord. I pray Almighty God that you will clothe my future husband with your love and power right now in Jesus name.

May your hands of peace and power always be upon his mind, soul, body and spirit. Lord, please help my future husband to feel your love and power. May he always give himself diligently in making his calling and dedication sure, in doing these things he will always be victorious in you dear Lord.

Lord, I pray for his mind and entire spirit. May the peace of God be in him. May he experience your power and love.

Heavenly Father may my future husband speak your word. May he be your oracle and mouth piece. I pray that his prayers will tear down Satan's schemes and territory in Jesus name. Please remind him dear Lord, that he is more than a conqueror through Jesus Christ who lives, move and breathe in him.

Dear Lord, please allow my future husband to put his validation in you and not in people. People's opinion and response to us will fail mighty God but help us to always count our opinion on you and seek your approval mighty God.

May all his desires be fulfilled through your divine process and in due season dear Lord, Lord, please don't allow us to keep waiting in vain dear Lord. Lord you see, we need to tie the knot but please help us to do in good season in Jesus name.

SEA OF OPPORTUNITY

Now unto him that is able to do exceeding abundantly above all that we ask or think, according to the power that worketh in us.

Ephesians 3: 20(KJV)

Prayer 38

Heavenly Father, I pray for peace of mind in body, soul and spirit this day in Jesus name. Lord, you said this is the day you have made and I will rejoice and be glad in it in Jesus name. Almighty God may your kingdom come today on earth as it is in heaven.

I pray for a continued renewed mind through your Holy spirit dear Lord. May you move, breathe and live in me this day and forever in Jesus name. Lord may every dead and difficult situation be cast into the sea of opportunity to rise and give you glory in Jesus name.

I thank you for the victory today, tomorrow and forever in your name. Amen.

DAILY GUIDANCE

Prayer 39

May Jehovah always be present in every dark and uncomfortable situation and emotion that we might experience in Jesus name. Heavenly Father, I pray that your hands of protection and provision will continue to extend as we seek your daily guidance for our lives.

Trust in the Lord with all your heart and lean not on your own understanding in all your ways acknowledge him and he will direct your path.

Today, Lord I felt you talking to me about my future husband, how to encourage and admonish him in the Lord. How to make him strong where all else seems gloomy.

Almighty Creator, I love creativity. Thank you for your gift and peace of mind today dear Lord.

THANKSGIVING

I will lift up mine eyes unto the hills, from whence cometh my help.

Psalms 121:1(KJV)

prayer 40

*D*earest Heavenly Father, I thank you that you came through for us during this extremely difficult situation. Lord, I pray that we would take all the lessons from this situation and use it to glorify you for being a promise and peace keeper in Jesus name.

We care not whether it goes against every details of our fibre. As long as we are walking in your precepts. Please give us the will, mindset and path to honour you with all our might.

Thank you for hearing and answering prayers. Thank you for the victory over everything that was weighing us down in Jesus name.

May we continue to lift our hands from where cometh our help. Lord, you are the maker of Heaven and earth, be exalted in all we do in Jesus name.

AGREEMENT

Can two walk together, except they be agreed?

Amos 3:3(KJV)

Prayer 41

Lord, I pray that as we prepare to share our lives together, we will both understand who we are in you. Help us to both live a life where we know that Jesus Christ is the author and finisher of our faith.

Heavenly Father, please help us to identify our purpose and calling in you before we say I do. Please help us to both be operating in our gift and calling and us joining together will be for the greater fulfilment of your purpose, where we will be encouraging and promoting the best and excellence in each other.

May we champion each other in love and mutual respect dear Lord. May we love each other than we do ourselves. May we always know and feel each other's love in Jesus name, I pray. Amen.

STRAIGHT AND NARROW

Prayer 42

Heavenly Father, I declare that my future husband will always have the mind of Christ in Him dear Lord.

Help him whenever he gets discouraged to always focus on the promises that you have rewarded to him, heavenly Father.

May you be all and more for him. May you always order his steps in your ways and set his path on the straight and narrow.

May whatsoever things that are lovely and of good report be his portion today and always in Jesus name.

FUTURE BOAZ

Prayer 43

Heavenly Father, Adam found Eve. May my King find me. He who finds a wife finds a good thing. Lord, I pray that you will open the eyes of my future Boaz, so he may see the Ruth in me. Lord, may my sacrifice and audacity of Esther be evident in my daily choice.

Lord, may your heart be compressed in my future husband, where his relationship with you deepens daily. May he be able to talk openly and honestly with you Dear Lord.

Heavenly Father may he know that what he has done does not define who he is.

Lord I pray that you will deal with the concerns and issues that are a catalyst and fear in his present thoughts and decisions. Lord please be the guide that shines through every dark corner of his life dear Lord, in Jesus name.

HEART OF GOD

Prayer 44

*M*ay the heart of God be at the centre of all

we do. Heavenly Father, I pray that the peace of God, the power and obedience of God's holy laws will be imprinted in our lives.

Heavenly Father, may we always be willing to sacrifice our desires for your divine purpose to be fulfilled. Please forgive us of our shortcomings oh God.

We have failed you on so many different events, but Lord forgive us our sins as we forgive those who also trespass against us.

Please, lead us not into temptation but please deliver us from evil. For thine is the kingdom, the power and all glory, amen and amen to you the Most High God.

NEW BEGINNING

My meditation of him shall be sweet: I will be glad in the LORD.

Psalms 104:34(KJV)

Prayer 45

*D*ear Heavenly Father,

It is always good to pray and not faint. Dear Heavenly Father, I pray that you will open the faith of our trust in you that we will truly challenge you and take you at your own word.

May the words of my mouth during this month and the meditation of our heart be acceptable in your sight oh Lord our strength and our redeemer.

GOD OF HEAVENS

Prayer 46

*Y*ou are God of the heavens

You are God of the earth

You are God of my heart

You are God of my hope

Forever you will be the one who reigns in our hearts

Heavenly Father, I live this day because you are making a way dear Lord.

You have reminded us time and time again to trust in you with all on heart, lean not on our own understanding in all – all – all- all our ways, we must acknowledge you and you in all your glory, in all you power , in all you your wisdom will grant us the desires that you have place in our hearts.

How much more should we not adore and fall in love with you, over and over again. Lord may our heart always be in tune with your desire for our lives in Jesus name.

INTERCESSION

For our God is a consuming fire.

Hebrews 12:29(KJV)

prayer 47

$\mathcal{H}$eavenly Father as I come to you right now

interceding on my future Husband's behalf.
Lord I pray that you will always keep him
under the shadow of your wings. Lord may his
ways always give you glory. Lord, you said the
steps of a righteous man are ordered by the
Lord. Lord may his steps always find favour
with you today.

Lord, if there are any areas that you need to
change, please show him where and how he
should change, any attitude or bad habits that
need changing. Please reveal to both of us
beforehand, so we can work and adjust these
before they are changed in Jesus name.

Lord, people sometime change when
circumstances arise but Lord, please I ask you
to help us to have the mind of Christ where we
love in season and out of season dear Lord.

Help us not to be a seasonal creature but
please help us to wear your humility, the fruit

of the spirit and the joy and power of your salvation.

Father help us to forgive and look beyond each other fault and always see the best in each other.

Dear Lord, please help us to see each other the way you truly value and love each of us, help us not to carry grudge or hatred, but to always have your peace and hope in our heart in Jesus name.

WEDDING DATE

*Two are better than one; because they have a
good reward for their labour.*

Ecclesiastes4:9(KJV)

Prayer 48

Thank you, heavenly Father that we have

agreed on a date. Lord we commit this day
before you. Heavenly Father may this day
honour you.

May this day be a day where the sun shines so
we can see your glory and majesty in our
marriage and in our lives.

Heavenly Father may our every decision be
favoured and honoured by you. I pray that you
will open closed doors to reason that we could
not even begin to imagine.

Lord send forth your Judah worship on our
wedding and marriage. I pray that we will
commit our finance to you, and we commit all
our days before you in Jesus name.

EFFECTIVE WORK

Prayer 49

*T*he words of God work effectively.

Heavenly Father, thank you again for life and care over us as we slept. That you for allowing the death angel to pass over us. Father, I place my future husband and I, our relationship present and future in your hand dear Lord.

I come against every judgement from each other. I bind every spirit of competition and comparison, right now in the name of Jesus to be silenced in Jesus name.

I come against any fake bridge of quarrel over minor matter to be dealt with effectively in Jesus name. May we be able to deal with our disagreements amicably in love, repent and through the direction of the Holy spirit in Jesus name.

I pray that no weapon formed against us will prosper in Jesus name..

Father, I pray that our conversation will be open and honest, as we deal with issues that we will face and find out about each other's perception on things dear Lord. May you always be at the centre in Jesus name.

- ❖ Child upbringing
- ❖ Christening
- ❖ Parties – Children parties
- ❖ Holiday
- ❖ Debt free
- ❖ Finance,
- ❖ These are things that cause relationships to break down.

We commit these aspects of our lives and everything that concerns us in Jesus name.

DISCERNMENT

Prayer 50

*P*rayer for humility and spirit of discernment concerning relationship with unsolicited member.

Heavenly Father, I pray that my future husband will always have the mind of Christ in him Lord. May his conversation always be full of substance and truth.

Spirit of the living God. I pray that you will breathe upon him, from the crown of his head to the sole of his feet. May his ways and desires always seek to please you dear Lord. Lord, please let your perfect will be done in Jesus name.

Lord, please speak clearly so he can hear and act upon your purpose for his clarity. I trust in your desires today and always knowing that you always know best.

FULFILMENT

Prayer 51

*H*eavenly Father; may your scripture, your word, come alive in us.

Take a woman and call her your wife, begin to fulfil your promise dear God.

The word "take" is a verb, hence an action word. This requires some movement in order to move from point A to B.

Daddy, I pray that these words will not be taken likely in Jesus name. May the deep understanding of this process be understood timely and clearly dear Lord.

Father, may this wait not be laborious, arduous and drawn out, where it becomes pointless and unbearable like a yoke dear Lord, because if the process seem arduous then, one might begin to think and feel misunderstood and unappreciated.

So, dear Lord I pray for honesty, tenacity and stalwart action, not to be weary before the right time is finished, in Jesus name.

OUR HELP

Prayer 52

*H*eavenly Father our help from who all age past. Our God and hope to come. Father, I lift my head to you right now, this very hour.

Please come and have your way in our daily lives dear Lord. May your countenance continue to radiate through our veins,

every decisions and paths that lay ahead.

Almighty God, please help us to study to show ourselves approved unto you dear Lord, rightly dividing the word of truth in our hearts and among those whom we encounter daily.

Please help us to be disciplined stewards of your word and your kingdom principles, dear Lord.

Please, forgive us of all unrighteousness. Dear Lord, help us to understand that two cannot walk unless they agree. Lord, I pray that your peace and favour will be with us all the days our lives.

SELFLESS LOVE

Prayer 53

*H*eavenly Father, you are love. No greater love that a man has for you that he should lay down his life for his friend. Thank you, Father, for your love.

Father, I pray that may future husband and I will be selfless as it relates to putting each other first in our marriage dear Lord. I know that you honour faithfulness, so dear Lord I pray spirit of the living God for you to consecrate us right now, to your will and to your ways. Help us to truly slain self and ensure that you reign supreme in all our ways and life dear Lord.

Lord, may your praise and thankfulness ever be upon our lips dear Lord. Heavenly Father, we love you.

SUCCESS AND FAILURE

Prayer 54

*H*eavenly Father as we enter a new year

Lord, I thank you for every success and failures last year. Thank you for the victories and revelation that you have shown us heavenly Father.

Lord, I pray that my future husband will always know that you are with him and he does not need to be afraid dear Lord. May you be his rock and his fortress in him.

Father, I pray that this year will be a year of opened doors and total surrender and obedience to things concerning his life Mighty God.

May you establish your kingdom here on earth as it is in heaven. Heavenly Father you say the kingdom of God suffered violence and violent take it by force, may he be found in your presence. May he be found fulfilling that which you have designed for him in Jesus name.

STEPPING OUT

Without faith it is impossible to please God.

Hebrew 11:6a

Prayer 55

Almighty God may this year be a year of

faith in action dear Lord. May we step out boldly and confidently through you Heavenly Father. May the peace of God that passes all understanding continue to rest remain and abide with us heavenly Father.

Father, may we multiply all the gifts and talents that you have placed in our care. Lord, may we truly know what we have in our hands Lord.

May we not bury our gifts but give us wisdom to go out and multiply for the kingdom of God. Father, I know that you desire for us to prosper in all things so heavenly Father please reveal yourself to us dear Lord.

Reveal yourself clearly to my future husband. May he know who he is in you mighty God. May you be everything and more to him. Be his confidant, be his provider, be his king of kings and Lord of Lords.

TONGUES OF FIRE

And there appeared unto them cloven tongues like as of fire, and it sat upon each of them.

Acts 2:3 (KJV)

Prayer 56

*H*eavenly Father, thank you for another morning in your presence. Almighty creator I thank you that you are establishing My future husband into you likeness. Please sit upon him like cloven tongue of fire dear Lord. Saturate him and bring out every negative and dark areas of his life that is hidden away from you.

May his crocked path be made straight. Mighty God, where there is procrastination, I pray for movement dear Lord.

I pray for action dear Lord. I pray for peace that surpasses all understanding to be upon him, all through his life heavenly Father. Please have your perfect way in him.

Lord, I pray that his actions will not bring you displeasure. Lord, may his actions please you in every way, may you reveal your purpose for our lives in your hand mighty God. Amen

PARTNERSHIP

Let nothing *be done* through strife or vainglory; but in lowliness of mind let each esteem other better than themselves.

Philippians 2:3(KJV)

Prayer 57

*H*eavenly Father, thank you for friendship and encouragement dear Lord. Thank you that you designed companionship to bring you glory and honour.

Lord, as we begin this partnership dear Lord please help us to esteem each other more highly, that we ought to think about ourselves.

Lord, please help us not to intentionally hurt each other. Please help us to be emotionally sensitive to each other's needs in Jesus name.

RIGHTEOUSNESS

Prayer 58

*H*eavenly Father, thank you for life and the
secret place that we are able to dwell. Thank
you for placing your light unto our path and a
light unto our feet Lord Jesus. Thank you that
because you are with us, we do not have to
fear or worry.

Heavenly Father, as we put on your robe of
righteousness and allow your word to dwell in
our hearts,

may we walk and operate with confident feet,
that only comes through trusting you.

Thank you for your presence and peace. As we
wait upon you, continue to have your way.
May our path always be clear before you, in
Jesus name.

KINGDOM COME

Prayer 59

*H*eavenly Father, may your kingdom come in my future husband's life this very moment in time Mighty God. Lord, you said before he calls, you will answer while he is yet praying and speaking, you will hear Almighty God.

Be his advocate now Lord. Give him exactly that which he needs to declare to your people in the morning as he leads prayer service.

Minister through him like an oracle from above Almighty God. Be his shield, protector in Jesus name, Amen.

THRONE ROOM

Prayer 60

*H*eavenly Father, thank you that you have

directed my future husband to your throne room. Thank you for his heart of gratitude to you dear Lord.

May you continue to smile upon him Almighty King. May you be the lifter of his head. May you be his righteousness dear Father. May you be his hope and glory.

May everything that has breathe praise the Lord. Lord, I decree that your kingdom will be established in him today and always.

As we visit the perspective sanctuary dear Lord. May our hearts be open up to your perfect will for our lives dear Lord.

Lord, I love you so much more and more. Love you today and always, Heavenly Father.

OUT OF DARKNESS

Prayer 61

*H*eavenly Father, thank you that you are

God of heaven and the earth. May your kingdom come on earth as it is in heaven today. Give us this day our daily bread Mighty God.

May your purpose and order for our lives be hidden and revealed in you righteous God. I decree and declare that your kingdom will come on earth as it is in heaven.

Heavenly Father may all the resources and legal attires, documents, mindset, protocol be in place long before we walk down and say: I do, Mighty God.

Heavenly Father, I fail to accept that you would have designed my life for me to almost spend my life this far alone. You said that you created both male and female.

You said a man should leave his Father and mother and cleave to his wife. You said a man shall take a woman and call her his wife.

Father, I pray that my future husband will be called out of darkness into your marvellous light Almighty God.

May you open the windows of heaven and clear the crooked path straight for him to move into his purpose and perfect will for marriage, in Jesus name.

SEEING ME

Prayer 62

*H*eavenly Father, I praise you mighty one, the maker and deliverer. I pray that as we prepare for marriage, Lord that we will not compare each other to others, who may or may not have been in our lives.

I pray that he will see that we are totally two different people and individuals and although from time to time it will be inevitable to still carry faith or remember routine that once was held dear and seemed as part of everyday life, to now let go and have a fresh outlook together as a couple.

Father, I pray that I will be seen and accepted through his eyes as you have accepted me. May he see me through your eyes mighty God. Father, may we see each other through your eyes heavenly Father. These I ask of you in Jesus Holy name.

ALL KNOWING GOD

Prayer 63

*H*eavenly Father, the one who sits high and looks low, the one who nothing in all creation is hidden.

Father, we pray and repent of every secret faults, sin and contempt in our hearts Lord Jesus. We uproot every seed of discontentment, fear, lack, worry, sickness and debt that has been planted or spoken over our lives in Jesus name.

Forgive us Lord, if we have held back that which is rightfully yours, help us to give to you that which is rightfully yours, help us to give to you our first fruits, tithe and our offering gladly in Jesus name.

Please help us to forgive others who has wronged us just as you forgive us in Jesus name.

Father we come against bitterness, anger, unforgiveness and malice in Jesus name. We will not allow the enemy to rob us of the blessings that God has ordered and designed for us in Jesus name.

DENYING THE FLESH

Prayer 64

*F*orgive us for the time that we have crossed
lines and fallen but help us to always have
confidence on every path that is laid before us.
Help us to exercise total confidence in you that
there is no dead thing in our lives. Breathe
fresh breath into our relationship in Jesus
name.

May all ungodly influence that is not beneficial
to us be extracted from our lives in Jesus
name.

Help us to never loose sight of the fact that we
have a mandate to fulfil in Jesus name.

May every temptation set before us be a sign
that you are with us and there is no
temptation presented that we are not able to
overcome.

Help us to remember that you have been tried,
proven, tested and came out as pure gold.
Help us to be blameless and faultless before
your throne.

Father, please help us to deny our flesh of the
temptations that will lead us against your
order and purpose for our lives. May we walk
according to the fruit of the spirit.

May we guard our heart and mind, may our mind be always clear. May our mind be always soaked with your words. May the peace and favour of God always be in our heart.

I rebuke evil, concubine, malicious, sexual predators and any other form of ungodly entities, spirits that want to attach their dirty, stingy self to us in Jesus name.

We pray for a discerning spirit to sense and pick up any of these concubine spirits from a far in Jesus name.

DRY BONES

Prayer 65

I call for our relationship, marriage to live in

Jesus name.

Heavenly Father, I prophesy over every dry bone in myself and my future husband's relationship Lord. Lord, I prophesy over My future husband's spirit like Ezekiel prophesied to the dry bones.

I command every purpose of God concerning your life, concerning my life to come to pass in this perfect season in Jesus name.

Wind of God blow upon the secret place of our relationship – breathe fresh breath, re-establish, send a renewing, send over flow in our relationship, ministry, gifting, finance, love, obedience, thanksgiving and thinking.

Whatsoever we speak may it come to pass in Jesus name. Whatsoever we ask for, it shall not be denied. God is about to blow in our finance. Blow in our income beyond measure.

Heavenly Father help us to sow in your court of your principles according to the principle of he word of God. May we walk according to the principle so we can receive our promise.

85

REVEALER OF SECRETS

Prayer 66

The king answered unto Daniel, and said, Of a truth it is, that your God is a God of gods, and a Lord of kings, and a revealer of secrets, seeing thou couldest reveal this secret.

Daniel 2:47 (KJV)

*H*eavenly Father, may My future husband know you as revealer of inner solutions for challenges that others in authority and his peers find challenging. May his faith in you draw them closer to you. To know of you, the God in whom he trusts and serve.

Give him an excellent and disciplined spirit and a positive work attitude dear Lord. Lord help us to be as disciplined as Daniel who prayed at least three times a day, morning, evening, now at night.

May we not bow to music of this world. May we not bow to society's expectation of our marriage, mat we not bow to the ways of the world.

Let your divine favour saturate every corner of our lives in Jesus name.

EXALTED

Prayer 67

Oh Lord, our God how excellent is your name. Father may your name be exalted in our lives, may your name be exalted in our families, may your name be exalted in our giving, may your name be exalted in our marriage.

May your name be exalted in our ministry, may your name be exalted in our health and strength, may your name be exalted in our worship, dance, prayer, admonishing, encouraging, teaching, preaching, worship, our everything in Jesus name.

FOOTSTOOL

The LORD said unto my Lord, Sit thou at my right hand, until I make thine enemies thy footstool.

The LORD shall send the rod of thy strength out of Zion: rule thou in the midst of thine enemies.

Psalms 110:1-2(KJV)

Prayer 68

Almighty Jehovah Elohim, Roi and El-Shaddai,

I thank you this morning for your loving kindness. Welcome into our prayer, welcome into our hearts, welcome in this place.

Holy one of Israel for that we honour you so much mighty Jehovah, you are the Most High God. Be exalted this day and forever in your heart.

Thank you for my future husband, may he know the strength, power and spiritual authority that you've placed in his hands. May we know that we are standing on the neck of our enemies.

They are our footstool; no scheme of men will be able to bulldoze us against the plans that Christ Jesus has for us. Thank Jehovah.

Thank you for the spirit of reconciliation heavenly Father. May your praise always be upon our lips in Jesus name. Love you so much dear Lord!

JEHOVAH ROI

Prayer 69

I bind every spirit that has aligned itself against our destiny for the kingdom of God to be uprooted and cast into the pit of hell in Jesus name.

My future life partner, husband, soul mate shall not be deceived or blinded by the plans (for) of the enemy to postpone, cancel, kill the plans that God has already destined in Jesus name.

Fire of the Holy Ghost go to the several places of his heart right now and minister your healing, minister to his suffering, minister to his emotions, minister to the hurt, minister to the broken spirit Almighty God.

I do not know if I am what he needs right now. He wants a quiet moment, but Heavenly Father be in his stillness dear Lord, please be in his quiet moment, may you please be in his quiet moment, may your peace that passes all understanding continue to keep his heart and mind at peace in Jesus name.

Thank you, Jehovah, that we are spiritually about to identify and pick up every satanic plans of the enemy. May the enemy's mouth be silenced right now in Jesus name.

The enemy will not use us against each other. The enemy will not use family or acquittances to cause disruption or ailment with the plan and purpose for our destiny in Jesus name.

Heavenly Father give us spiritual wisdom to handle every phase of courtship, marriage and disagreement in Jesus name. May our hearts be one for you in Jesus name. The enemy will not be able to use others, family, relatives, finance against us in Jesus name.

FEAR OF THE LORD

Let us hear the conclusion of the whole matter: fear God and keep his commandments; for this is the whole duty of man."

Ecclesiastes 12:13 (KJV)

Prayer 70-

*H*eavenly Father, may our desire always be found in you daily. May we cause our faith to look to you. May we be totally surrendered to you Almighty God.

Show us supernatural things that we need to operate here on earth to cause others to see your glory and wonders through us Almighty God. Jehovah, you are the Most High God, be exalted oh Lord.

Help us not to delay things. Help us not to keep carrying things over dear Father. Help us to understand that you are the way, the truth and that no one comes to the Father except by you.

Heavenly Father help us to deliver to you our thinking about things that does not concern us or things that will not bring you glory oh Lord. Lord, bind up every bond of wickedness against us in Jesus name.

Father, we choose life today. We choose your blessings of Abraham Almighty God. We choose to live for you and obey your voice that makes the difference Lord.

Heavenly Father, may your peace that passes all understanding continue to keep our hearts and minds through Jesus Christ. We love you this day and forever more, Amen!

UNQUENCHABLE

Many waters cannot quench love, neither can the flood drown it, if a man would give all the substance of his house for love, it would utterly be condemned

Solomon 8:7 (KJV)

Prayer 71

Mighty waters cannot extinguish love, rivers cannot sweep it away.

NET BIBLE

Surging water cannot quench love flood waters cannot overflow it.

God's word translation

Raging water cannot extinguish love, rivers will never wash it away.

*H*eavenly Father, thank you for the conditions that we have found in the counsel of your word. 'hank you for spiritual marriage counsellor who is feeding into our relationship mighty God. Thank you for Godly counsel

May you continue to pour more of your spirit upon us oh God. May we choose people who will invest and pray over our relationship in Jesus name. May your blessings be for us today and always.

RHEMA WORD

In the last days your sons and daughters will prophesy.

Joel 1:8(KJV)

Prayer 72

*H*eavenly Father, give us a Rhema word for today Lord. Give us an active word for what you need us to do in our relationship Almighty God. Help us to be faithful in our conversation and in our giving. Help us to be ministers of our finances in Jesus name. Lord please help me to give to you what is rightfully yours in Jesus name, Amen.

Lord, I pray that my husband will wear the Armor of you daily. May his head and mind be guarded by supernatural outflow of prophetic words.

We know that the weapon of our warfare is not carnal but is mighty through the pulling down of strong holds. Thank you Jesus, for pulling down strong holds in Jesus name. I love you so much Jesus.

Who so findeth a wife findeth a good thing and obtained favour of the Lord.

Proverbs 18:22(KJV)

Favour is from those who seek it from the God.

Let there be mutual submission between both of us. Help us to learn to say sorry to one another whenever we wrong each other Lord.

Ephesians 5:22   May the Lord preserve our union, our home, our children, our ministry, our life, our possession and our love.

ABUNDANT LIFE

Prayer 73

A happier mood brings benefit beyond feeling good. Happiness has been linked to better physical health, higher income, greater relationship satisfaction.

Heavenly Father, you said that my future husband and I should have life and have it more abundantly.

Lord, I pray that we will always be naturally generous people dear Lord.

I pray for our health Lord Jesus, that we will be healthy and wealthy people in the kingdom. May we have enough to give to others. May we be faithful in our tithings and giving dear Lord.

Thank you for your abundant life dear Father. May all our ways acknowledge your Mighty and awesome power dear Lord.

FRUITFULNESS

"Be fruitful and multiply"

Let us make man in our image. Let them have dominion on the earth.

Genesis 1:26(KJV)

Prayer 74

Heavenly Father, thank you for the dominion that you have placed in My future husband and I life. Please help us to understand the purpose of our destiny in Jesus name.

God needs my future husband and I: to impact lives, our family, our children, our nation. God needs a human. We must always pray and never faint. I have given you the key to heaven, whatsoever we loose on earth Jesus Christ will loose.

Our body is the most important thing to you oh God right now. God, you cannot act on earth without a body. God heals us because he needs our body not because he wants us to feel good but so that we can be better for his purpose.

Our body is important to God. The same spirit that raised Jesus Christ from the dead will live in our mortal body, use us for your glory Lord.

LOVE IS KIND

Prayer 75

*H*eavenly Father, thank you for my fiancé.

Thank you for his heart, thank you for his mind, thank you for his hands, thank you for his feet, thank you for his arms, legs, eyes, ears, his mouth, his tongue, his lips, his feet. Thank you for the heart and mind that he has for you.

Lord I thank you for creating my future husband in your own image oh Lord. Thank you for the original purpose that you have for his life.

Thank you for making him perfect for me oh Lord. May his heart always be loving and committed to you and may his heart be guided by your principles in Jesus name.

BLAMELESS

That ye may approve things that are excellent. That ye may be sincere and without offence till the day of Christ. Being called with the fruit of righteousness which are by Jesus Christ, into the glory and presence of God.

Philippians 1:10 (KJV)

Prayer 76

Heavenly Father, I pray that my future husband will be blameless and will be innocent of any offence Lord.

May your purpose and divine will be fulfilled in our lives Almighty God, Amen.

CHRIST'S LOVE

So, ought men to love their wives as their own bodies. He that loveth his wife loveth himself. For no man ever said he hated his own flesh; but nourished and cherished it, even as the Lord to the Church.

Ephesians 5:27-28(KJV)

Prayer 77

*H*eavenly Father, I pray that my future husband's heart will be always open to this kind of love in our marriage dear Lord.

Please help us to wear this love every single day of our life. May we know, feel, experience, see, hear, taste, smell and celebrate each other's love in your sweet Holy name.

Prayer 78

May we model this kind of love to our children, siblings, brothers, sisters, strangers, to the world, to our enemies, to those who speak against us in your sweet Holy name.

Help us to love you with all our heart, all our mind and all our soul, as we seek to worship you in spirit and in truth. We love and adore you Almighty God.

HANDS OF GOD

"Hide me from the secret plot of the wicked, from the rebellion of the workers of iniquity who sharpen their tongue like a sword and bend their bows to shoot their arrow-bitter words".

Psalm 64:2-3(KJV)

Prayer 79

*H*eavenly Father, our help through ages past, our hope to come. I place the life of my future husband and I in your hands, oh Lord.

Lord, I understand truly that you hate divorce because it goes against your original intention of mankind and for the family. But Lord Jesus I ask you to have mercy dear Lord. Please do not cast me away from your presence.

Please do not take your Holy Spirit away from us dear Lord, renew unto us the joy of your salvation and renew a right spirit within us.

Heavenly Father, please allow your words to be upon our hearts. Dear Lord, please draw us to your cleansing power. May your infinite wisdom continue to draw us under your mighty hands.

Help us not to accept or receive ill advise or counsel from those who do not understand your principles and purpose.

Lord, we just want to commit our all to you in Jesus name I pray. Amen.

PROPHESY

Again he said unto me, Prophesy upon these bones, and say unto them, O ye dry bones, hear the word of the LORD. Thus saith the Lord GOD unto these bones; Behold, I will cause breath to enter into you, and ye shall live:

Ezekiel 37:4-5(KJV)

Prayer 80

Heavenly Father I pray that my future husband will be able to speak, prophecy your word over every dead bones in his life right now and hereafter in Jesus name.

May we know the hope of your calling and the power of your word.

Heavenly Father strengthen his faith in you right now dear Lord, allow him to experience the joy of your anointed hands.

We offer our thanksgiving for breathing life, hope and restoration into our future in Jesus name, amen.

WILDERNESS PRAYER

But the hour cometh, and now is, when the true worshippers shall worship the Father in spirit and in truth: for the Father seeketh such to worship him.

John 4:23 (KJV)

Prayer 81

*F*ather, may my future husband and I understand the hour and our season. May we hear your voice in our different season Lord. In the good time, not so good time, the afflicted time; may we hear you in our wilderness experience.

May our ears be open completely to your voice so we can discern what you are saying to us in Jesus name I pray.

Thank you Lord Jesus be glorified in Jesus name.

Help us not to wait 40 years or 40 days in the wilderness; you only spent 40 days. The children of Israel spent 40 years because they refused to listen and obey you. May we obey and hear your clearly, dear Lord, amen.

DIFFICULT

prayer 82

Lord Jesus my heart is broken today Lord

two people who I love dearly are in Turmoil
Lord. Often times misunderstanding can
confront and presents itself in a way that
seems right in both parties' eyes. But Lord, I
pray that you will be the mediator, right now,
in Jesus name.

May every stronghold come down right now in
Jesus name. I pray that you will go ahead and
chop down every wheat that wants to stifle the
presence of your shekinah glory in every
moment of our lives.

Lord, so far this has been one of the most
difficult of period to date this year.

May the praise of your kingdom be established
on earth as it is in heaven dear Lord.

Lord I pray that you will be the calming water
to our stormy sea today, may you be the water
that quenches our soul with an abundant
overflow of your grace.

Heavenly Father, I pray that you will supply all
the love and forgiveness that we hold dear to
our heart dear Lord.

Father please help us to be wise, help us to be the salt and light of this world, may everyone see the Joy, peace, love and righteousness in the Holy Ghost, Dear Lord.

May we know that you have called us to bring Joy to the people, not hurt, not pain, not judgement, but to show forth the glory of God in all of us.

Evening, and morning, and at noon, will I pray, and cry aloud: and he shall hear my voice

Psalms 55:17(KJV)

TRANSFORMED

And let the beauty of the LORD our God be upon us: and establish thou the work of our hands upon us; yea, the work of our hands establish thou it.

Psalm 90:17(KJV)

Prayer 83

*H*eavenly Father please continue to protect my future husband's heart dear Lord. May his heart be transformed into your likeness.

Please hide him under the secret place of your most high. May he love the things that you love. May he humble himself before you. In Jesus Holy name.

THE KING OF GLORY

Prayer 84

Heavenly Father,

I present the life of my future husband and I before you this morning please reveal to us through your word – through your prophet, through your holy spirit – your perfect will for our life Lord. Heavenly Father, please help us to know and obey your word only. Please do not cause your face to turn away in anger.

Father may every plan that we have come together according to your perfect will. Dear Lord- please help us to understand the deep – thoughts of your heart beat for us Lord- help us to identify every spirit that come to steal, rob and destroy all that you have for us king of glory- be magnified. Dear Lord come in king of glory, come in!

FLOURISHING

The word of God is a lamp unto my feet and a light unto my path

Psalm 119:5 (KJV)

Prayer 85

*H*eavenly Father. This day I present to you

Lord –saying that we love you Lord more than we do ourselves. We offer you all of our heart, we offer you all of our praise, be thou glorified holy God.

Lord may your word be so hidden in our heart, so that we will not sin against you, oh Lord. Lord we know that you desire truth in the inward part. The inward part is the part that others cannot see Lord- Father take residency there.

Lord as your word fall on our ground, Lord, may our ground be fertile ground, where plant can grow and flourish, dear Lord. Please do not allow the harsh season of life to destroy the seed that you have placed in us Lord. May we water these seed Lord daily that we may bear fruit in due season in Jesus name.

SANCTIFY

Prayer 86

Lord, I place my future husband before you,

right now and ask you to sanctify him with your truth and grace.

May your desires be manifested in every area of his life, mighty God.

Lord may our courtship bring you glory dear Lord. Lord I place every thought or concern, that we are concerned with, before you mighty Lord.

Lord where there is uncertainty give us clarity – where there is blurred vision and mist – wash it so it can be clear – send your rain, send your fresh water to clear the path that is unclear before us. Fresh insight /fresh revelation.

May your perfect will continue to be done in our lives in Jesus name amen.

UNDERSTANDING

Prayer 87

*H*eavenly Father- Thank you for my future husband and his children Almighty God. Lord, these 3 people will become a part of my family dear Lord, help us to get together as a unit Almighty Lord.

Please help us to begin to see how we react together as family and dear Lord. Help us to be loving and respectful to each other.

Please help us to be good role models with each other. Please help us to teach our children boundaries, help my future husband and I to frame new experience with patience, resilience and love.

Please, help us to understand each other's love language dear Lord – please help me to respect and listen to my future husband – help my future husband to be patient, generous and successful father and husband in Jesus name.

ACTIVATE

Prayer 88

Heavenly Father, I thank you in advance for favour Lord God, for our lives in Jesus name.

Thank you for establishing your kingdom in the life of my future husband and I. Thank you for opening your kingdom door unto us, heavenly Father. May all that we are be in you God.

Thank you for speaking to my future husband today about writing down vision and make it plain, so he can see it, others can see it and he can begin to activate, the actions and the faith in order for the word to come to fruition and bear fruit Almighty God. Heavenly Father - thank you for extending your mercies to us dear Lord.

May we get in line, may we stay in line may all areas of our heart and mind be in line from this day forward in Jesus name.

Lord we surrender all that we are before you, our future plan for marriage and our daily walk with you, be it on our Easter break, dear Lord. We have two weeks of Easter please help me to spend my time wisely dear Lord.

PERFECT WILL

But the Comforter, which is the Holy Ghost, whom the Father will send in my name, he shall teach you all things, and bring all things to your remembrance, whatsoever I have said unto you.

John 14:26(KJV)

Prayer 89

*D*addy Jesus – I surrender all to you mighty one. We surrender our heart, our desires, our will and our ways to you.

We ask you to lead my future husband and I into your truth. Please help us to operate from a higher level – where we don't allow the lies of the enemy to ruin what you have already deposited into our hearts, oh God.

Father the things that I have no control over mighty one; help me to cover and surrender it all to you. Lord I pray that these areas of our lives that are outside of our control. We surrender to your perfect will and way mighty God.

I pray that you will help us to deal with any trials and tribulation that want to present its head in our journey in Jesus name I pray amen.

MEEK

Now the man Moses was very meek, above all the men which were upon the face of the earth.

Number 12:3(KJV)

Prayer 90

*H*e visited then in the tabernacle of meeting, where He revealed himself in the pillar of cloud and spoke to Moses and siblings.

Heavenly Father, may my future husband's heart be one of total surrender and humility before you Lord.

I pray Lord God that we will not be disobedient in our walk with you, like the children of Israel who murmured and forgot all that you have done in your deliverance of them.

Heavenly Father, please order our daily steps dear Lord – help us to act knowing that you are watching us, knowing that you are mindful of us, knowing that you have called us out of darkness into your marvellous light. Heavenly Father help us to be in accordance with your will mighty God.

TEMPLE OF GOD

For this is the will of God, even your sanctification, that ye should abstain from fornication: That every one of you should know how to possess his vessel in sanctification and honour; Not in the lust of concupiscence, even as the Gentiles which know not God:

1Thessalonican 4:3-5(KJV)

Prayer 91

*H*eavenly Father – may my future husband

and I keep our bodies as temple and living sacrifice for your glory. Help us to be vessel of honour ready to be used by your perfect will dear Lord.

I pray that we will know that obedience is better than sacrifice dear Lord. I give you praise and thanks Heavenly Father.

We commit all our preparation, plan, finance and conversation and decisions, both here and in the future to you in Jesus name dear Lord.

ATTITUDE OF PRAYER

but as for me and my house, we will serve the LORD.

Joshua 24:15b (KJV)

Prayer 92

Help My future husband dear Father to keep you at the centre of his heart and decision. May his heart be open to your will and to your ways.

We pray for holiness, righteousness and sanctification in our lives in Jesus name.

We call every dry bone to come into alignment in Jesus name.

I speak to every dry bone in our lives to come alive in Jesus name.

BETTER THAN SACRIFICE

"Behold, obey is better than sacrifice, and heed than the fat of rams"

1samuel 15:22b (KJV)

Prayer 93

Heavenly Father may we be obedient to every single promise and move of your Spirit in our lives dear Lord.

Please help us not to choose things that you have clearly instructed us to abstain and not get entangled with Lord.

Please help us to be free from all immorality of the flesh, spirit and movement in Jesus name. I speak life into every dead situation and circumstance that wants to engulf us right now in Jesus name.

May your kingdom come into our heart on earth as it is in heaven – amen.

WAYS OF MAN

Lord I know that the way of man is not in himself, it is not in man that walketh to direct his step.

Jeremiah 10:23(KJV)

Prayer 94

Heavenly Father – Holy one of Israel please direct my future husband's footsteps dear Lord – lead him to his wealthy place – spiritual, emotionally, physically, financially, professionally and intellectually dear Lord.

Please order every one of my future husband's decision making – may his ways be favoured in your sight dear Lord. Renew the joy of his salvation – renew a right spirit within him- cast your presence not away from him but lead him into your path of right standing with you heavenly Father.

May our love continue to grow stronger because many deep waters cannot quench this love.

SHADOW OF GOD

He that dwelleth in the secret place of the most High shall abide under the shadow of the Almighty.

psalm 91:1(KJV)

Prayer 95

*D*ear Lord – may my future husband always hide under your shadows mighty God – give your angel charge over him Almighty one.

Because you oh Lord has set your love upon my future Husband, therefore, you will deliver him may he set you high above all and everything, oh God. because he knows the power and assurance of your sovereignty.

May the joy of your salvation always be his strength.

Strengthen and sustain him dear Father, order everything that concerns him this day and always in Jesus name.

BIRTHDAY PRAYER

Prayer 96

Heavenly Father thank you for setting your zeal upon my future husband, may your powerful hand rest upon him with all your strength.

When he is hurt and despondent, comfort him with your powerful hands. May your peace continue to rest, remain and abide with him today and forever, dear Lord.

Birth in him your Chenaniah dear Lord (ken-ani-ah) a Levite leader of the house of Obed-Edom

May every thoughts and assignment sent out toward him be dismantle through the praises of his prayer and worship to you.

May he remember who and whose he is, in Jesus name.

Lord when the enemy comes in like a flood, please continue to lift your standard, heavenly Father against him. In Jesus name.

UNITY AND SURRENDER

Prayer 97

*H*eavenly Father, you oh Lord determine the end from the beginning according to Isiah 46:10

You oh God determine the end from the beginning, so Almighty God I pray, that as I minister to you with my heart, you will open up the flood gates of heaven and shower your peace on me dear Lord. Please let your will be done Almighty God, let your will be done in our lives, order our steps before you dear Lord.

Help us to walk in your precept – remove blind spots from our eyes dear Lord, every scale that lays naked in our heart. Let your will be done I pray in Jesus name.

MARRIAGE SCRIPTURE

As we prepare for marriage.

Therefore shall a man leave his father and his mother, and shall cleave unto his wife: and they shall be one flesh.

Genesis 2:24(KJV)

Many waters cannot quench love, neither can the floods drown it: if *a* man would give all the substance of his house for love, it would utterly be contemned.

Solomon 8: 7(KJV)

Husbands, love your wives, even as Christ also loved the church, and gave himself for it;

Ephesians 5: 25(KJV)

For thy Maker *is* thine husband; the LORD of hosts *is* his name; and thy Redeemer the Holy One of Israel; The God of the whole earth shall he be called.

Isaiah 54:5(KJV)

(Son 8:6) Set me as a seal upon thine heart, as a seal upon thine arm: for love *is* strong as death; jealousy *is* cruel as the grave: the coals thereof *are* coals of fire, *which hath a* most vehement flame.

(Son 8:7) Many waters cannot quench love, neither can the floods drown it: if *a* man would give all the substance of his house for love, it would utterly be contemned.

Song of Solomon 8:6-7(KJV)

PREPARATION TO MARRIAGE

For God, who commanded the light to shine out of darkness, hath shined in our hearts, to give the light of the knowledge of the glory of God in the face of Jesus Christ.

2 Corinthians 4:6(KJV)

Prayer 99

Thank you, Jesus, for victory over oppressed mind and spirit. Father open our eyes, so we may see wonderful things in your truth and your word.

Heavenly Father – may you shine over every areas of my future husband's heart, so those areas that are hurting and broken can be restored – may your favour and peace continue to illuminate in every area of his life in Jesus name. –

Dear heavenly Father, be the way maker in every oppressive spirit, may we find you always in our heart and mind in Jesus name.

FAMILY MEETING

And said, If thou wilt diligently hearken to the voice of the LORD thy God, and wilt do that which is right in his sight, and wilt give ear to his commandments, and keep all his statutes, I will put none of these diseases upon thee, which I have brought upon the Egyptians: for I am the LORD that healeth thee.

Exodus 15:26(KJV)

Prayer 100

Heavenly Father, as my future husband meet my parent and some family members Lord. I pray that your healing balm in Gilead, will bring restoration and deliverance where hurt and pain has taken up residence.

Lord, send forth your Judah and your Jehovah rapha power to administer your dosage of healing and restoration right now in Jesus name.

I am anticipating your miracle and victory every step of the way- I prove you Lord, you said in your word to prove you now, so let me prove you always as my king – I love you today and forever in Jesus name.

AUTHOR AND FINISHER

*H*eavenly Father – thanks, that you have declared in your word that a righteous man is cautious in friendship.

Lord you also declare in proverbs 13: 3. *He who guard his lips guard his life but he who speak rashly will come to ruin.*

Almighty Father I pray that my future husband and my soul mate will carry your Spirit with him in every situation, Dear Lord. –

May he stand assured that you Jesus, are able to do for him exceedingly abundantly all that he can ask or imagine.

May the joy of the Lord be his mouth piece that when he opens up his mouth to speak – he will speak like an oracle Almighty God – be his friend and shield.

Father, burn out all pride that can cause and breed quarrels, let wisdom be found in the advice that is presented in love according to your word Almighty God.

Lord I pray that we will be able to have good understanding with matters concerning each other, ourselves and others dear Lord.

– Lord you said that good understanding wins favour, so let your favour penetrate every area of our lives, give us godly tolerance to let go of people who might have hurt us, speaking ill and have poor intension for our lives.

Lord may your word be the final authority on which we build our marriage in Jesus name please help us to see you, as one who is the author and finisher of our lives. Amen!

WALKING WISDOM

Whoso despiseth the word shall be destroyed: but he that feareth the commandment shall be rewarded.

Proverbs 13: 13(KJV)

Father you've declared that he who walketh with the wise grows wise, but a companion of fools suffers harm.

Misfortune pursues the sinner, but prosperity is the reward of the righteous

Heavenly Father –please let your will be done Almighty Jehovah as we take on each other's life and we join to become one with my future husband, please help us to get our lives and heart in order before we are joined together,

help us to set our path – help us to create an atmosphere of trust with finances, family affairs, hopes, dream and our expectation as we celebrate and appreciate our lives with each other, Lord.

I have 8 weeks to get things in order – please help me to prioritize important plans and the Journey ahead, thank you Lord for hearing and answering in Jesus name.

HEALING WOUNDS

He healeth the broken in heart, and bindeth up their wounds.

Psalms 147:3(KJV)

*A*lmighty Jehovah you are the mender of broken heart, we commit every thought and emotions to you dear Lord, for you to turn on your spot light on us in Jesus name.

You ask if there is anything that is too hard for you – no, not one, nothing under the sun is difficult for you.

So right now, I place my future husband and life partner into your capable hands, for you to mend, heal, hold and break according to your likeness in Jesus name. Please continue to order every details of his life according to your perfect will Jehovah.

Lord I thank you that you are the discerner of the intents of the heart. Thank you for your release dear Lord. Thank you for allowing your sweet spirit to minister to my future husband in his quiet time and his public life.

Thank you for not allowing him to lean unto his own understanding dear Lord, - thank you for the shift that you have started Almighty Jehovah. We trust and hope in you today and always amen.

JUDGE NOT

(Mat 7:1) Judge not, that ye be not judged.

(Mat 7:2) For with what judgment ye judge, ye shall be judged: and with what measure ye mete, it shall be measured to you again.

(Mat 7:3) And why beholdest thou the mote that is in thy brother's eye, but considerest not the beam that is in thine own eye?

(Mat 7:4) Or how wilt thou say to thy brother, Let me pull out the mote out of thine eye; and, behold, a beam *is* in thine own eye?

(Mat 7:5) Thou hypocrite, first cast out the beam out of thine own eye; and then shalt thou see clearly to cast out the mote out of thy brother's eye.

Mathew 7:1-5(KJV)

*H*eavenly Father I pray that my future husband's heart will always be tender toward me dear Lord.

May his love for me never die or goes weary. May he never question his decision, your decision and our decision to be joined together Almighty Lord. Lord I know that there will be some challenges ahead, but Lord help us to remember that you have already made a plan and a way for us to overcome. You said that you will not allow the enemy to consume or overtake us. Lord we want to see your glory working in our lives. We desire to be the agent of change for you and in you Almighty one. Abba Father we set our hearts on fire for you.

Help us to be honest and open without condemnation or being judgmental of each other. Help us to be obedient to you Lord in our foundation of loving you, thank you for answering this prayer in Jesus name.

FINISHED DESTINY

The LORD will perfect *that which* concerneth me: thy mercy, O LORD, *endureth* for ever: forsake not the works of thine own hands.

psalm 138:8(KJV)

Your destiny is established and finished according to Myles Munroe. You are the process towards your end, God is committed to your destiny.

*H*eavenly Father thank you that you are committed to our destiny in Jesus name. Thank you that you are committed to the very small details of our lives, let your will be done. Almighty God – may your kingdom be established in every details of our paths.

Help us to pray for every single person in the corner of our lives Lord – everyone that you have caused to make us fall on our paths – every one who you have caused to be a thorn, a rose, calming seas or treacherous waters and everything combined. Thank you for your sweet smelling fragrance – beautiful one in Jesus name

(Psa 32:7) Thou *art* my hiding place; thou shalt preserve me from trouble; thou shalt compass me about with songs of deliverance. Selah.

(Psa 32:8) I will instruct thee and teach thee in the way which thou shalt go: I will guide thee with mine eye.

Psalm 32-7-8(KJV)

(Mat 5:23) Therefore if thou bring thy gift to the altar, and there rememberest that thy brother hath ought against thee;

(Mat 5:24) Leave there thy gift before the altar, and go thy way; first be reconciled to thy brother, and then come and offer thy gift.

Mathew 5:23-24(KJV)

STRATEGIC ORDER

*O*rder every one of my future husband's step in the name of Jesus; order his life – order his decision – health, profession, decision, finances, home, whole past, present, future, relationship, friendship , conversations ,prayer, praise, intercession, fasting, love, forgiveness, hope, strength, love for me, love for you, love for his children, order his leadership, his home and his family, his life – those who are over him and under him in Jesus name.

DOWN THE AISLE

Today I walk down the aisle and I declare my undying love for you mi Amor. Thank you for loving me, thank you for choosing me to be your good gift, you are my good thing.

May our hearts always be in love and presentable before each other and to the Lord our maker today and always, love you forever. My darling husband.

Printed in Great Britain
by Amazon

40655572R00076